The HOLY CRY

Dr. D. K. Olukoya

HOLY CRY

Dr. D. K. Olukoya
MFM Ministries
Nigeria

Holy Cry

1st Printing - January, 1999

2nd Printing - October, 2009

ISBN 978-2947-54-7
©1999 Mountain of Fire and Miracles Ministries

All rights reserved. Reproduction in whole or part without written permission is prohibited.
Printed in Nigeria.

All Scripture is from the King James Version

Cover Illustration: Sister Shade Olukoya

Published by MFM Ministries
13, Olasimbo Street, off Olumo Road, Onike
P.O. Box 2990, Sabo, Yaba,
Tel: 01-868766, Lagos, Nigeria.
E-mail: mfm@micro.com.ng.
mfm@nigol.net.ng.

Design, type-setting and printing
MFM Press
13, Olasimbo Street, Onike,
Yaba, Lagos.

Other Publications By MFM Ministries
- Students In The School Of Fear
- The Vagabond Spirit
- Power Must Change Hands
- Breakthrough Prayers For Business Professionals
- Pray Your Way To Breakthroughs (Third Edition)
- Spiritual Warfare And The Home
- Victory Over Satanic Dreams (Second Edition)
- Personal Spiritual Check-Up
- Prayers That Bring Miracles (In English, Hausa, Igbo & Yoruba Languages - 1996 Seventy Days Fasting Prayer)
- "Adura Agbayori" (Yoruba Version of the Second Edition of Pray Your Way To Breakthroughs)
- How To Obtain Personal Deliverance (Second Edition)
- Power Against Local Wickedness
- Brokenness
- Let God Answer By Fire (1997 Seventy Days Fasting & Prayer Programme in English, French, Hausa, Igbo and Yoruba Languages)
- Release From Destructive Covenants
- Prayers To Mount Up With Wings As Eagles (1998 Seventy Days Fasting & Prayer Programme in English, French, Hausa, Igbo and Yoruba Languages)

TABLE OF CONTENTS

Chapter 1
The Cry Of The Human Heart — 1

Chapter 2
The Holy Cry — 7

Chapter 3
Examples In The Scripture — 19

Chapter 4
Men And Women Who Cried Unto God — 34

Chapter 5
Forty Holy Cry Prayer Points — 51

chapter 1

THE CRY OF THE HUMAN HEART

Let us start this message by taking the following prayer points:

1. I refuse to be in the tail position, in the name of Jesus.
2. Let every spirit of the valley attached to my life be disgraced, in the name of Jesus.
3. Every battle working against my life, be crushed, in the name of Jesus.
4. Let progress, success and breakthrough pursue and over take me, in the name of Jesus.
5. Every power that has converted my life into a market place, be wiped out by the Holy Ghost, in the name of Jesus (take this particular prayer point for some three minutes, then begin to say: Be wiped out, in the name of Jesus. Don't forget to keep your right hand on your head as

you take this prayer point and expect the manifestation of the Holy Ghost).

6. Every satanic cage, be roasted by fire, in the name of Jesus.

7. Every spirit working against my life from ..., fall down and die, in the name of Jesus (place the name of your town or village in the space provided above).

God is all wise and all knowing. In His omnipotence, He created a vacuum in the heart of man which makes everyone to yearn for help from above.

Every man, irrespective of academic attainment, financial ability and intellectual achievement experiences trying moments in life. Great achievers are known to have experienced moments of anxiety, despair, bewilderment and total resignation to fate. Great men have experienced total helplessness in their sober moments. Millionaires have wept like babies when they discovered that money could not solve all their problems. Scholars, thinkers, technocrats and consultants have tried to fight back the tears that welled up from within the inner recesses of their hearts. Renown celebrities, especially the names which we have all grown up to respect have also had their moments of perplexity.

As a minister, I have counseled hundreds of great men and women who have distinguished themselves in their various careers. I have been surprised sometime, when I listened to heart-rending stories from men and women who are exceptionally talented.

I have also wondered in my heart of hearts why university professors, international business men and women, top military officers, first class traditional rulers, seasoned diplomats, brilliant consultants, successful researchers, respected politicians, top government functionaries and people whose assets run into millions of dollars steal in spite of their unique achievements.

Sometimes I have had to go back to my prayer closet to worship the most high for His omnipotence and supremacy over man. My experience in the ministry has made me to conclude that God is indeed, the Ancient of days.

I have discovered beyond every shadow of doubt that God is the 'All Sufficient One' and that man at his best is altogether vanity. What would you do, for example if a Nuclear Scientist whose name rings a bell in the International Academy of Science comes to you weeping and telling you that his world has been turned up-side down.

What would you do as a minister of God? How would you feel if it turns out that the scriptures already have solutions to such a person's problems. "O the depth of the riches both of the wisdom and knowledge of God! How unsearchable are his judgments, and his ways past finding out! For who hath known the mind of the Lord? Or who hath been his counsellor?" (Romans 11:33-34).

THE VACUUM

Man is incurably dependent on God. Give a business man all the money in the world and you will discover that you have not solved all his problems. Give a housewife everything money can buy, you will discover that her heart is still yearning for fulfillment. Give a student all the academic degrees that can be obtained and you will discover that great learning or education is no substitute to total fulfillment in life. Give political power to a politician he will discover that power is insatiable.

There are many people who were in the corridors of power but became empty afterwards. Money does not satisfy and power cannot replace God. Success cannot fill the God-shaped vacuum in the heart of man, pleasure too is transient, it has no enduring value. The heart of man is divinely crafted by the Almighty in such a way that there is a spontaneous cry which erupts each time man is at his wit's end. That cry can be likened to an automatic signal which comes up whenever the sensor which is resident in every man detects a problem which is beyond human ability.

But may I ask? Who does not cry? A cry is an automatic response to a situation which looks disturbing, a feeling which appears overwhelming, a thought which seems weighty or a condition that has remained unpleasant. Crying is natural but it is a pity that a lot of people cry out their hearts to no avail. I pity women who have formed the habit of crying at the dead hours of the night just because they do not know what to do with their problems. To cry in despair without knowing how to get divine solution to life's problems is to waste your tears. Those who cry because they are discouraged or to give vent to their emotions are only operating in the physical realm. Shedding tears or crying as a human being cannot paralyse the activities of the devil. So, you need to know how to cry in a positive sense and attract divine attention.

chapter ii

THE HOLY CRY

This book centers on the kind of cry that attracts heaven's attention. I want to show you how to turn your cares, anxieties, deepest desires, burdens and urgent needs into prayers that can not be denied. There is a kind of cry which strikes a chord in the heart of our Father God. When you understand how to cry unto the Lord and make heaven to stand at attention and respond promptly, fully and miraculously to your need then you understand holy cry. When you understand and begin to put this kind of prayer to use, you will begin to experience wonderful results in prayer.

You will also discover that there is a level in spiritual warfare where your holy cries can send jitters into the camp of the enemy. When you cry unto God for divine intervention, judgment against the enemy, release of what the enemy has stolen from you, restoration of the ground which you have ignorantly shifted to the enemy and a stoppage of all forms of demonic harassment, you will experience amazing results.

THORNS IN SATAN'S FLESH

The devil dreads the cry of saints who know their God. The Bible does not say that, "Those who know their God shall be weak and shall be exploited." The only cry which the devil is afraid of is the aggressive cry of trained warriors.

The devil hates the holy cry. It sends spine-chilling shocks into his system. The cry of embattled and angry prayer addicts threatens the camp of the devil. It works against satan's camp like volcanic eruptions.

When Christians who are on fire cry unto the Lord, the devil gets mad. To cry unto God against the power of darkness is to destroy the works of the devil. The power that is resident in the warrior's cry is inestimable. Only heaven can quantify the amount of battle that has been won, the number of destiny that has been restored, the number of deliverance which God has granted helpless victims of demonic manipulation and the amount of hopeless cases which have received divine touch.

Perhaps, what your present situation needs may be a holy cry which puts a final full-stop to the activities of the devil in any life. Give it a try and your life will not be the same again.

Indeed, God's ways are past finding out. He uses foolish things to confound the wise. He also uses simple actions to confuse the devil. Sometimes, God uses a simple action of faith to achieve what fasting has failed to achieve. You can send a holy cry to heaven when you are angry with the devil as a result of his interference in your life. You can cry against demonic injustice and you can raise your voice like thunder against every enemy that has ever attempted to make your life a dumping ground for all kinds of problems that are fabricated in evil factories. You can also cry and shout as an inhabitant of Zion against every uprising from the kingdom of Babylon.

Beloved, it is shouting time. This is the hour of high pitch praying. This is the moment when the devil should be able to recognise your voice and tremble. The battle has entered top gear. The days of cowering and cringing before the devil are over. We have entered the season of dominion. The time when a believer should become a threat to devil as a result of the holy cry which the believers utter. This is God's emphasis for now.

SCRIPTURAL FOUNDATION

Let us examine the scriptural foundation for holy cry. To do this we shall examine some scriptures which bear relevance to the understanding of our subject. The scriptures are taken from the book of Psalms:

"When I cry unto thee, then shall my enemies turn back. This I know for God is for me" (Psalm 56:9).

"Out of the depths have I cried unto thee, O Lord. Lord, hear my voice; let thine ears be attentive to the voice of my supplications" (Psalm 130:1-2).

These two references have a lot to say concerning holy cry. They teach us that there are times and seasons when men and women are supposed to cry unto the Lord.

Holy cry comes as a result of a number of reasons. It is possible that you are familiar with the holy cry in your own experience. For most people who are sincere, down to earth and practical, holy cry is a common experience. Men and women cry unto the Lord for a number of reasons:

ONE, they cry unto the Lord because of the burdens in their hearts. It is not always easy for a man who has serious burdens to pray mechanically.

TWO, men cry out of desperation. Again this is a common human experience. A man who is at his wit's end will generally experience such a feeling with tears, not with carefully selected and well articulated high sounding speech. Have you ever seen a man who is weighed down by despair? Such a man will surely resort to the use of holy cry in expressing himself before the Lord.

THREE, holy cry is also used by God's people to express anger against their enemies. The man who is angry cannot speak gentle words. When you are angry with the devil and his agents you have to cry unto the Lord.

FOUR, holy cry comes during drastic situations. It is difficult to predict human response during drastic situations. A cry is natural during emergency situations.

FIVE, since human experience differs from one person to another, holy cry often comes with spontaneity. There are times when we often find ourselves crying unto the Lord without any form of premeditation. So, it becomes clear in view of this and other reasons that holy cry is a normal human response to diverse situations. It shows our dependence on the Lord, our faith in Him, our human weakness and the unpredictable nature of life. To cry unto the Lord is to appeal to the courts of heaven and to call for divine intervention in your situation.

A UNIVERSAL PHENOMENON

Why should a man cry? That is a normal question which I expect any one to ask. Crying is universal. It emanates from all men in all nations. A cry goes out from human beings from time to time, from the cradle to the grave. Take a look at a new born baby. As soon as he is born, he cries out. That is a sign that a living child has been born. If a new born baby fails to cry, then something is wrong somewhere. How do we interpret the cry of a new born baby?

ONE, the baby could be crying because he feels that he is starting a journey into trouble and crisis.

TWO, it could be in response to a rough expulsion from a place of comfort to a place of discomfort. In any case, it is not a comfortable cry.

It is clear that such a cry is not supposed to come out in one's life again, except one comes under severe attack. After this stage, such a cry is abnormal. When a man cries out then you know that something has gone wrong somewhere.

Jesus knows that the life of a man will be filled with rough experiences which will make him to cry. That is why he substituted for us by crying on the cross. Jesus sounded a note of finality on the problems that will make us to cry when he cried out and said, "It is finished." Jesus substitutionary cry has put a stop to our personal problems. Legally, two people are not supposed to cry over a single crisis. Since Jesus has done all the necessary crying, we need to appropriate our blessings now. That is why any power militating against any true child of God is looking for trouble. Such powers are looking for what I call evil substitution. They will be pursued by terrifying noises.

MEN WHO DARED GOD

God is a God of judgement. He is always tough and does not spare those who desire to fight against Him. If you take a look at history, you will discover that everyone who dared God paid great prices.

Emperor Nero was one of the most wicked men who ever lived. He fought against Christianity with all his might. He paid dearly for it. He died a miserable death. Voltaire was one of most popular French men that ever lived. He once vowed to devote all his energy to ensure that every Bible in France was destroyed. He vigorously pursued that decision but he later died. Printing was invented after his death. Then the unexpected happened. A Christian press bought Voltaire's house and started to print Bibles there. That was how the house of the man who wanted to destroy the Bible began to house one of the greatest presses where Bibles were printed in Europe.

Let me state once again that any power militating against any child of God is seeking for compulsory burial like Korah, Dathan and Abiram.

Adolf Hitler was another man who tried to raise his head against God. He was so proud and arrogant that he decided to declare an open war against God and His people. He failed. He was so hated that school children were later taught to sing against him. He vowed to capture Africa and turn it to a rubber plantation. He also had a morbid hatred for Christianity. He was referred to as the Anti-Christ. Today, Hitler is dead and forgotten. His headquarters in Berlin has been turned to a Christian chapel. Hitler was not alone in his hatred for Christianity. One of his closest aides, Martin Bowman, called Christianity a poison and warned his wife never to allow his children to swallow such a poison.

Again, Martin Bowman died and seven out of his nine children became Christians. In fact, one of them even became a missionary. This shows that any one who tries to wage war against the true child of God is seeking to be eaten by spiritual worms after the order of Herod.

A group of demonic agents decided to attack a Christian gathering. One of them was charged with the responsibility of carrying out the attack. This person who happened to be the chief demonic agent had a powerful charm in his pocket. The plan was that the charm was supposed to be thrown at the preacher to cause confusion. They entered the Christian gathering and took their seats pretending to be church members. Everything had been calculated.

When it was time to strike, the evil messengers exchanged glances, then the chief agent knew that it was time to strike. He put his hands into his pocket to bring out the charm but to his amazement his hands got stuck to his pocket. He struggled and struggled but his hands were glued there. When his friends found out that he was slow in doing what they had all planned together, they shouted at him telling him that time was going. Then they came nearer and discovered that something was wrong with him.

They started running away one by one leaving him alone. He continued to struggle with the charm in his pocket, making several efforts to free his hands from his pocket, but nothing worked. Having been abandoned by his friends, it dawned on him that he was in serious trouble. He reasoned that the best thing to do was to surrender, if not his condition would remain like that forever. He rushed forward when the altar call was given.

A minister sensed the predicament of the demonic agent and decided to help him bring out his hands from his pocket. He decided to expose himself and told the minister that he had actually come to attack the man of God. He began to cry telling everyone that he was sorry for ever attempting to attack the servant of the Lord. That was how he was set free.

chapter iii

EXAMPLES IN THE SCRIPTURE

To utter holy cry unto the Lord, you must get to a point where you can say: "Enough is enough." When you get to a point where you are ready to face satan and his agents and tell them that enough is enough, you will discover that they will no longer be able to keep you in bondage. You will not tolerate whatever is unpleasant from the camp of the enemy.

On many occasions in the Bible, there were people who felt that their problems had come to a climax and they cried out saying: "Enough is enough." A look at the Bible and contemporary experience show that those whose problems have come up to the brim often received their miracles. The reason is not far-fetched. A man who has gone to the end of the road, having no where else to turn to, will look up to God with desperation. A man who is tired of the topsy-turvy conditions of life will not pray sluggishly. Such people will cry unto the

Lord from the depth of their hearts. Such cry always receives instant attention from God.

This is a kind of cry which God never rejects. God is a loving Father. He cannot stand our cry of desperation. His heart is so tender and full of pity that when we cry unto Him, He rises to the occasion with the fullness of His power, love, compassion, grace, provision, protection, deliverance, and mercy. The reason most of us are still smarting under hostility is because we have not discovered the power that resides in the holy cry.

If certain situations in your life refuse to change, it is probably because you have never applied the power of holy cry to it. But if you utter holy cry unto the Lord you can be very sure that heaven will respond. The total manifestations may not be known to you but God has answered all the same. The ways of God are unfathomable. He works in ways we cannot see. When He makes ways in the wilderness, sons of men sometimes think that they are still walking through the wilderness.

Perhaps, you have uttered some fervent holy cry unto the Lord thinking that He did not respond. May be, He has responded and you have not been able to identify the miracle.

GOD IS A WAY

May I tell you this today, God has set your miracle in motion if you have truly uttered the holy cry unto Him. The children of Israel cried unto the Lord but they did not know that their cry initiated a lot of miraculous manifestations. They cried when they were under bondage in Egypt, God responded to their cry in a very different way.

The miracle of the children of Israel started with the burning bush. You may ask: What has the burning bush got to do with bondage and servitude? In human estimation, nothing. But according to divine economy, that was the beginning of their miracles. The burning bush was highly symbolic. It was God's message to Israel showing them that they would triumph in spite of their crisis.

Human opinion is many miles away from what God does so many times. If as a human being you happen to have just listened to the cry of the children of Israel expecting God to respond immediately and you walked passed them the next moment only to see a burning bush, you will not be able link the two events. Unknown to the children of Israel the answer to their prayer has started with the burning bush. While God was looking at the beginning of their miracles they were still looking at their bondage.

Unknown to you the answer to your prayer might have started in England. Right now, who knows God would have also raised up someone in far way U. S. A. in response to your holy cry. God will bring the miracle to you or He may link the two together in His time. You may not be able to relate what is happening to your present situation. But I speak to you prophetically. "There shall be a divine connection very soon."

Your burning bush will become a stepping stone to your deliverance, breakthrough, prosperity and success. Do not write yourself off. Do not limit yourself in life.

Your present condition will not be permanent. Poverty will not remain with you permanently. You will not remain a permanent deliverance candidate. God will bring a change to your life. He will hearken to your cry and wipe your tears away. He will cut the shackles of bondage and set you free. He will take you from Egypt and place you in your own Canaan, the land flowing with milk and honey. God will rewrite your history and change your destiny. I speak to you as a servant of the Most High, your cry has attracted divine attention. God has already dispatched angels on assignment to you.

He has already signed some documents towards your promotion. You are in for a change. Your miracle is settled in heaven. God will lift you from the dunghill to the throne. He will transform from you being a Mr. NOBODY to a Mr. SOMEBODY. You will graduate from the position of a beggar to a giver, instead of being dependent on people you will become somebody on whom other people will depend.

EXPECT A MIRACLE

A single cry can change your life. We can cry one day and a situation that has remained persistently stubborn will change in one split second. If a barren woman utters a holy cry, she can become a joyful mother. A poor man who cries unto the Lord will become a rich man.

When a man whose condition is completely hopeless cries unto God for divine intervention, he will become hopeful. There are cases of people who got to the point of committing suicide, but cried unto God in their helpless state and received instant help from above.

Again, there are people who had been written off by society but experienced great changes after crying unto the Lord. I know a particular case of a member of the church who had to be given regular financial assistance by the church, because there was no help from any other source. He cried unto the Lord and the situation changed. Today, he is a millionaire. God changed his status as a beggar to the elevated position of a comfortable man by all standards.

From the foregoing, you can see that a single cry unto the Lord can change your life for good. Your history can be rewritten by one single holy cry. Your life can become a wonder to all if only you cry unto the Lord today.

LESSONS FROM THE BIBLE

What lesson can we learn from those who cried unto the Lord in the Bible? A lot. When we examine the situation of men and women who passed through the same circumstances which we are passing through today, we will be encouraged by the amazing manner with which the Lord change their circumstances.

There is an encouraging story in the twenty-sixth chapter of the book of Genesis. The story is centered on the life of Jacob. Surprisingly, Jacob happens to be a classical example of what it means to have a crisis.

There are people today who feel that their problems are the greatest.

There are also people today who feel that ending it all is the only option. Sad to say, there are people who have committed suicide just when they are about to experience great changes in their lives. The changes came anyhow, but they did not live to enjoy them. It is never wise to conclude that all hope is lost. No matter what your yesterday and today look like, you cannot give up on yourself.

There is a bright new tomorrow for you. If God can change the situation of a man like Jacob, He will do the same for you.

God has used Jacob's case to tell us that: No matter how bad your situation is, there is hope. One of the things that has continued to baffle men and women is the fact that God always handles impossible situation with ease. He has handled countless number of impossible cases and turned them to miracles.

Let me ask you: What kind of man was Jacob? He was a man who did not qualify for any miracle. He was in a total mess. If God could be called the God of Jacob, in spite of all his shortcomings, then God can be called your God too.

Let us take a look at verse 26: "And he said, let me go for the day breaketh and he said I will not let thee go except thou bless me."

Jacob had thought that he had come to the end of the road with no where to turn to except to the hills from where cometh his help, he held on to God with desperation. He told the angel, "I won't let you go, except you bless me." But may we ask: With what power did Jacob hold down the Angel? How was a man able to wrestle with an Angel and prevailed over him?

It has remained a mystery up till now. Indeed the power of prayer is unfathomable. Jacob had only one prayer point and he handled that prayer point from around 10.00 p.m. in the night till 5.00 a.m. the next morning. He spent seven hours with God, crying unto Him. Jacob prayed without giving in to tiredness. He refused to budge even when the Angel said: "Let me go."

The dislocation of his leg did not move him, he was desperate. Being tired of his situation, he was not ready to take 'no' for an answer. For Jacob, it was a do or die matter. He was not ready to accept an unpleasant situation as the will of God. He was tired of persistent problems, harassment by his enemies, unsettled life and all forms of problems which the devil had engineered. He cried for hours telling God just one thing. He wanted blessings at all costs.

Jacob did the unusual, he handled one prayer point for seven hours and received an extraordinary blessing from God. He suffered a minor dislocation, yet that did not disturb him. Many of us cannot pray when everything around us is alright, not to talk of praying under great pain. Jacob was in great pain, yet he prayed.

Have you ever suffered dislocation, or broken an arm or a leg? Then you will know what it means to suffer acute pain. While blood was perhaps gushing out from Jacob's knees or while he was writhing in pains, he cried unto God the more.

Have you ever watched a boxing tournament? Have you ever seen somebody who was knocked down with blood all over him? It takes a great resolve for such a person to continue fighting. Jacob appeared knocked down by the Angel, yet he continued fighting. At the end he prevailed.

The reason many of us do not prevail is because we give up too soon. A little delay, we get tired. A little disappointment we turn back saying, we have had enough. If Jacob had given up after six hours, he would have lost the greatest opportunity of his life. Good enough, you have fasted for two days, or you have prayed for two hours. But until you get to the last lap of the battle, you may never know what it means to experience victory and triumph. Jacob fought the battle to the last point. He refused to give up until he got the desires of his heart.

Today, many of us have refused to take after Jacob's example. Many of us are too lazy. We pray for one hour and we are tired. Today, many have developed a phobia for fasting.

There are people who cannot even fast from morning till 6.00 p.m in the evening. There are people who think that they will die if they fast for one full day. There are people who rush to quickly break their fast before time because of one little noise in their stomach. There are also people who are expected to fast for two days, but they had never attempted such a fast because of fear.

There are no miracles today, because many people are not prepared to pay the price. Jacob experienced a great change in his life because he cried unto God for seven hours. If you were in Jacob's shoes, won't you go about complaining and blaming God for your problems?

Jacob's holy cry was: "I will not let you go, except you bless me." I am yet to see a man who will cry unto God in that manner and fail to get results. Jacob succeeded because he vowed that he would not rest until his problems received a final full stop from the hands of God.

When I see people going through problems today, I wonder if they can cry unto God like Jacob did. Many people want their pastors to pray for them. Yes, your pastor can pray for you but there are certain problems in your life which you need to take to God on your own. Jacob did not rely on any one to pray for him. His life had been filled with problems. His situation at that time, was nothing to write home about. His future was uncertain. He packed everything aside and decided to tackle his problems once for all. He did not care if he was going to lose his voice. He did not care about sleep. His problems were burning him like fire, hence nothing mattered to him but his resolve to receive divine intervention.

After seven hours of handling one single prayer point, he got the attention of God. Problems are not good. But I know that there are people who cannot pray seriously unless there are problems in their lives.

The Angel responded to Jacob's problems. He stretched forth his hands and uprooted Jacob's problems in all its entirety. The Angel asked him, "What is your name?" Jacob answered. The Angel told him, "Thy name shall no longer be called Jacob but Israel." And from that moment, the life of Jacob changed. But why did the Angel change Jacob's name? The reasons are obvious.

There are times people's conditions cannot be changed totally except their names are changed. There are people who do not understand us when we say that people's names can affect them negatively. God wanted to change Jacob's life. He had to change the old name which had become part and parcel of the old conditions. He had to give him a new name in order to reflect the new dispensation which he was getting into.

Perhaps something is wrong with your name. You may have to cry unto God to experience a change of name; which will bring a change of life.

chapter iv

MEN AND WOMEN WHO CRIED UNTO GOD

There are lots of challenging examples and instances of men who cried unto God and had their lives changed for good. I am sure you can discover your own kind of situation in what they went through. If you can cry unto God like these people did, you will also experience a miraculous transformation in your life. Let us look at Exodus 17:4, "And Moses cried unto the Lord saying, what shall I do unto these people, they be almost ready to stone me."

Moses got to a situation in his life when he felt threatened. The children of Israel were mad at him and wanted to stone him. He had no option but to cry unto God. The reason many of us pray gentle prayer is because we are at ease in Zion.

A man who is comfortable will generally not feel like crying unto God. If everything around you is calm and quiet, you can pray for five minutes and doze off. But if the roof above your head is burning, you cannot pray like a gentle man. Bring a man face to face with a situation that threatens his very existence and he will never pray quietly.

He will shout with holy madness. He will cry unto God like a man who is hedged in from every angle by hostile forces. Out of desperation, Moses cried unto the Lord. It was not a time to recite the Lord's prayer, nor was it the time to say the grace.

If you were in Moses's shoe, you would not be able to recite prayers that are written in the book of common prayers or recite some lithurgy.

To cry unto the Lord means to pray from the depth of your heart and with every energy that you have in you. Moses cried out unto God. The situation around him brought out an emergency cry from him. The Lord hearkened unto his cry and gave him a prescription which brought an end to the threatening situation.

If you can cry unto the Lord today, He will also give you a prescription which will put an end to your unfavourable situations. Numbers 12:13 centres on another cry unto the Lord by Moses.

"And Moses cried unto the Lord, saying, heal her now, O God, I beseech thee."

That was indeed a very short prayer, but it was a heartfelt cry unto the Lord. Many people's conditions have remained the same, because they have not discovered what it means to cry unto the Lord.

There are people who have carried heavy loads on their heads for twenty years and above simply because they have never cried unto their Lord. Again, there are people who have allowed sicknesses in their bodies for more than ten years because they have failed to cry unto God for healing. There are many people who have continuously faced financial embarrassment because of failure to cry unto God for prosperity. Unless you cry unto God, your situation will remain unpleasant.

There is another instructive example in 1 Kings 17:20-22; "And he cried unto the Lord, and said, O Lord my God, hast thou also brought evil upon the widow with whom I sojourn, by slaying her son? And he stretched himself upon the child three times and cried unto the Lord, and said, O Lord my God, I pray thee, let this child's soul come into him again. And the Lord heard the voice of Elijah."

Here, Elijah the man of God was still staying with a family and the only child of the woman who had been playing hostess to Elijah died suddenly. Elijah rose to the occasion by crying to the Lord. He prayed with holy anger and asked the Lord to restore the boy's life. How do you pray if you have to raise a dead boy to life? Will you pray quietly? No, you will cry and shout because you are angry as a result of what the devil has done.

There are many situations in our lives which requires the kind of holy cry which Elijah uttered in his situation. Elijah was not conscious of the fact that his crying was embarrassing. Verse 27 tells us that God heard Elijah's cry and the dead boy was raised to life. The impossible became possible because Elijah cried unto the Lord. Cry unto God today and you will experience a great change in your life.

FROM SORROW TO GLORY

After spending many years in the ministry, I have come to discover that no matter how bad any situation is, it will change if only you can cry unto God. As I read the Bible, I have discovered that the type of situations which many complained are impossible are the type which Bible characters changed through crying unto God. One incident which is more striking than any other in the scripture is the situation of Jabez. Jabez was the worst man I ever came across in the scripture. He was a total write off. His background was a completely negative one. His situation was so pitiable that people called him sorrow. His story is recorded in I Chronicles 4:9-10,

"And Jabez was more honourable than his brethren: and his mother called his name, Jabez, saying, because I bare him in sorrow. Jabez cried out to the God of Israel saying, Oh that thou wouldest bless me indeed, and enlarge my coast...," And God granted him his request."

Jabez must have surveyed his entire life and must have been tired of everything. He decided to cry unto God. Are you like Jabez? Have you lived in sorrow? Are you so poor that people can make you a reference point as far as poverty is concerned? I have good news for you. All you need to do is cry unto the Lord. If you can cry unto the Lord today, you will experience a great change like Jabez. You will become honourable. You will be lifted from a lower position in life to a position of great honour. There is no shortcut to divine breakthrough. To refuse to pray is to remain in a hopeless condition. The man who can cry unto God has hope. God will grant your request if you can cry unto Him today.

NEW TESTAMENT EXAMPLES

The holy cry is not limited to the Old Testament. There are instances of men and women who cried unto God in the New Testament. One of such cries can be found in Matthew 14:30: "But when he saw the wind boisterous he was afraid and beginning to sink. He cried, saying, Lord, save me."

Here, Peter was between life and death and there was no one to turn to. He cried unto God. Are you sinking in the sea of life? Is your life threatened by great crisis? Are you at a point where your life is almost taken away by powers of darkness? Then you have no option but to cry unto God. Peter cried unto the Lord when he found out that the wind was contrary and he was sinking. The Lord rescued him. God expects you to cry unto Him whenever your life is threatened in any way. He will rescue you.

The next example is a woman who cried out in her desperate situation.

"And, behold, a woman of Canaan came out of the same coast and cried unto him saying, have mercy on me O Lord, Thou son of David. My daughter is grievously vexed with a devil" (Matthew 15:22).

This woman cried unto God on behalf of her possessed daughter. The situation touched her heart and she turned the burden into a holy cry. She cried until the Lord answered her. Verse 23 tells us that Jesus did not even answer her immediately. His disciples told Him to send her away. Jesus dismissed her saying, "I was only sent to the lost sheep of the house of Israel." But the poor woman did not stop crying. She stood her ground and gave reasons why she must get a response to her holy cry. At the end she won. Her cry attracted divine attention.

We have another pathetic situation in Mark chapter 9: "And straightaway the father of the child cried out, and said with tears, Lord, I believe; help thou my unbelief" (verse 24).

The holy cry we have just read came out from the father who was concerned about his epileptic son. Having witnessed a lot of domestic accidents, the father decided to make use of the opportunity he had. He decided to cry unto Jesus. He was tired of watching his child knocked down here and there, time and again, by epilepsy. He wanted healing at all cost. He cried unto God and received his miracle.

BLIND BARTIMAEUS

Perhaps the most striking incident of holy cry in the New Testament is 'Blind Bartimaeus.' I wish Christians can pray like Bartimaeus. Here was a man who had lived with blindness all his life. He had one single chance and decided to make the best use of it. He put all energy into prayer because he had no other option. It is difficult for people who have other options to pray with all their energy. Bartimaeus made his prayer a do or die affair.

"And when he heard that it was Jesus of Nazareth, he began to cry out and say, Jesus, thou son of David, have mercy on me" (Mark 10:47).

He took a single prayer point repeatedly, shouting at the top of his voice. Let us look at verse 48: "Many rebuked him and told him to hold his peace, but he shouted the more saying Jesus son of David have mercy on me."

At that point Jesus called on him. The people who had shouted him down were the same people who, according to verse 49, told him, "Be of good cheer. Arise, he calleth thee."

That was how Bartimaeus became free from the yoke of blindness. Don't allow people's comments to hinder you from crying out to the Lord. If you stop crying to the Lord because of criticism, you are not wise. Those who criticise you will also turn around and praise you when you experience divine blessing. In any case, those who criticise you will call you a foolish man who was not persistent in prayer.

Have you cried unto the Lord like Bartimaeus? Is there any tincture of aggression or desperation in your prayers? Can you hold on to the same prayer point in the face of ridicule from enemies and scoffers? Are you ready to take the same prayer points until the answer comes? Then you are ready for a miracle.

From the foregoing, one thing becomes clear, those who cry to the Lord always get results. I am yet to see one man who cried unto the Lord and did not receive a miracle. What lessons can we draw, therefore, from these examples of holy cries:

1. **People cry unto the Lord out of desperation**

When a man or a woman is desperate the result is a cry of desperation. Several people have asked me how easy it is to get delivered? I have always given them one simple answer. The moment you become desperate your deliverance becomes easy. Can you imagine someone who decides to address a stubborn demon sluggishly saying "You-the--owner---of---- evil-----load------carry-------your--------evil---------load,-------

---in-----------Jesus'-------------name.--------------A--m--e--n.

The demon will just laugh at such a careless prayer. That is a sign of not being serious in prayer. But when you become desperate your prayer will be red hot.

2. **All these people uttered holy cry unto the Lord.**

Hell knew that they were praying. Heaven also recognised that some people were bombarding it's doors with holy cries. Although we've done a lot of praying at the Mountain of Fire and Miracles Ministries, but I have always compared my personal perception of praying with our prayer efforts so far and have come up with this conclusion; we have just begun to pray. I look forward to a greater dimension of prayer. I have been praying about a day when our corporate and personal prayer lives will reach a higher dimension. I believe that we shall soon enter a new phase of aggressive prayer.

THE APOSTLE OF PRAYER

I have read many books on prayer, deliverance and spiritual warfare. I have also listened to challenging testimonies concerning men and women who attained unusual height in prayer. There is one testimony that has continued to challenge me.

J. A. Babalola, a foremost pioneer of African Pentecostalism prayed in a unique way. To him, praying was like breathing. He surpassed his contemporaries in the ministry of prayer. I am yet to encounter somebody whose prayer life can surpass that of Apostle Babalola. The stories of his prayer life often sound unbelievable to ignorant students in the school of prayer. For example, we heard from authentic sources that there was one instance when this respected Apostle of prayer was handling the prayer requests of his followers at the top of a popular Nigerian prayer mountain.

It was said that his adherents had dropped their prayer requests in a basket. According to the story, this man of God lifted up the basket and cried unto the Lord saying, "Father, behold the prayer requests of your children. Come down from heaven answer by fire." He had not finished praying when fire descended from above and burnt all the prayer request papers leaving the basket untouched. Everybody was surprised. That was how holy cry from a man like you and me brought real fire from heaven.

If that story sound challenging to you let me give you another one. A story has it that Apostle Babalola visited a particular family and decided to lead their regular evening devotional prayer. The family in question did not bargain for anything beyond their family altar. Pa Babalola began to pray and continued without stopping. An hour passed, the second hour passed, Apostle Babalola continued. Soon all the children fell asleep, the adults too started falling asleep.

After some five hours, Apostle Babalola was the only one who was praying. The fact that there was no sound of Amen to support his prayer did not stop him from praying. The family woke up the next morning and were surprised to discover that the visiting Apostle was still praying as if he had just started a few minutes ago. The members of the family who ought to go to work left him behind. They came back in the evening and met him on his feet the way he was praying the previous night. That was how he continued praying until he had prayed for seventy two hours. He started praying around 9.00 p.m. On Sunday and by the time he said a closing "In Jesus name, I pray", it was Wednesday evening. What a prayer giant!

You may ask, was he not tired? How could a man stand on his feet for three days? What of hunger? What did he have to say for seventy two hours? No doubt, these are elementary questions. You must pray that God should take you into a new realm where prayer becomes a second nature. The surprising thing is that by the time the Apostle finished praying, he apologised for prolonging the evening prayer a little longer and then told them to go and sleep. They all laughed at him and told him, "Sir you have prayed for three days. We left you most of the time and have been going about our normal duties. Today is not Sunday, but Wednesday. You have been standing on your feet praying for three days." That was how that family came face to face with a prayer prodigy. They learned what it means to pray and utter holy cry unto the Lord. The Apostle did not feel that anything unusual had happened. He was as fresh as he was when he started praying.

He was no doubt fed with heavenly bread. He also received supernatural strength to stand on his feet for three days without breaking down.

3. **The prayer of these people were very short, concentrated and direct.**

You do not need to impress God with long grammar. Unnecessary display of ornate, flowery and high-sounding language cannot give you a miracle. Just go to God and tell him in a few words. If you have ever used our book 'PRAY YOUR WAY TO BREAKTHROUGHS,' you would have discovered that the prayer points are short and direct. We have testimonies from every part of the globe concerning miraculous manifestations of the power of God in the lives of those who use the prayer points.

4. The cries of these Bible characters brought results.

It is very easy to condemn those who cry unto the Lord, but the results gotten by them are indisputable. If your prayer methods have not given you tangible results you better forget them and learn to pray like these men and women. If you begin to cry unto God like them you will also get similar result.

5. These people were discouraged by those around them.

For most of them, their kind of prayer brought sharp criticism from fellow neighbours. But they were resilient.

chapter v

FORTY HOLY CRY PRAYER POINTS

The scriptures examined in this book can be converted to forty holy cry prayer points. These prayer points will demolish any mountain, bring deliverance to the captives, break stubborn yokes, destroy satanic weapons and put a full stop to every form of satanic harassment. You can take these prayer points with fasting, night vigils and holy aggression and you will experience unprecedented miracles. Below are the life changing prayer points:

1. Let the angel of my blessings locate me, in the name of Jesus.

2. The angel of my blessings will not go unless he blesses me, in the name of Jesus.

3. Let my cry provoke angelic violence, in the name of Jesus.

4. Lord, give me the name that will bless me, in Jesus's name.

5. My cry shall touch heaven today, in the name of Jesus.

6. Every avenger circulating my name, be silenced, in the name of Jesus.

7. Every pride of the enemy, be disgraced, in the name of Jesus.

8. Every evil pattern in my family, be powerless against me, in the name of Jesus.

9. Every evil reporter, receive blindness, in the name of Jesus.

10. Every satanic hindrance targeted against the angels of my blessings, be dissolved by fire, in the name of Jesus.

11. O Lord, deliver me from evil stones thrown at me by unfriendly friends, in the name of Jesus.

12. Every evil riot and rage against me, be disgraced, in the name of Jesus.

13. Oh Lord, deliver me from every satanic noise, in Jesus' name.

14. Let every evil crowd seeking my life, be scattered unto desolation, in the name of Jesus.

15. Let every sickness in my body come out with all its roots, in the name of Jesus.

16. You poison of sickness, be drained out of my system, in the name of Jesus.

17. Every abnormality in my body, receive divine healing, in the name of Jesus.

18. Every fountain of infirmity, dry up, in the name of Jesus.

19. Every hunter of my health, be disappointed, in Jesus' name.

20. Every stubborn pursuer of my health, fall down and die, in the name of Jesus.

21. My head will not be anchored to any evil, in the name of Jesus.

22. Let evil pursue all unrepentant evil workers, in the name of Jesus.

23. I neutralise every power of satanic strategy, in Jesus' name.

24. No evil shall overtake me, in the name of Jesus.

25. Let every dead area of my life receive resurrection power of the Lord Jesus Christ, in the name of Jesus.

26. Oh Lord, enlarge my coast, in the name of Jesus.

27. I command every satanic embargo on my progress to fall down and scatter, in the name of Jesus.

28. Let God manifest His power against my oppressors, in the name of Jesus.

29. Oh Lord, don't be a spectator in my affair, in the name Jesus.

30. Oh Lord, anchor Your mercy to my head, in Jesus' name.

31. Oh Lord, let it be known that You are God in every department of my life, in the name of Jesus.

32. Oh Lord, let the earth open and swallow every stubborn power that is pursuing me, in the name of Jesus.

33. Oh Lord, let every rage of the enemy against me be quenched, in Jesus' name.

34. Oh Lord, answer me by fire and roast every evil strong hold in my life, in the name of Jesus.

35. No evil shall overtake me, in the name of Jesus.

36. I release myself from failure at the edge of success, in the name of Jesus.

37. My testimony will not vanish, in the name of Jesus.

38. I paralyse every spirit of wastage and I shall not borrow, in the name of Jesus.

39. All my hardened enemies, receive confusion and disagreement, in the name of Jesus.

40. I break every covenant formed against me by the enemies, in the name of Jesus.

Books in this series

- Revoking Evil Decrees
- Power Against Spiritual Terrorists
- Wealth Must Change Hands
- The Great Deliverance
- Deliverance For The Head
- Power Against Coffin spirits
- Limiting God

To order for the tape of this message,
"Holy Cry"
write to or call at
MFM Tapes Ministry,
13, Olasimbo Street, Onike, Yaba,
☎ 01-868766 Lagos.

MFM and The AUTHOR

Dr. D. K. Olukoya is the General Overseer of the Mountain of Fire and Miracles Ministries. He holds a first class Honours Degree in Microbiology from University of Lagos, Nigeria and a Ph.D. In Molecular Genetics from The University of Reading, United Kingdom. As a researcher, he has over seventy scientific publications to his credit. Anointed by God, Dr. Olukoya is a Teacher, Prophet, Evangelist and Preacher of the Word. His life and that of his wife Shade, are living testimonies that all power belongs to God.

Mountain of Fire and Miracles Ministries, is a ministry devoted to the revival of Apostolic signs, Holy Ghost fireworks and the unlimited demonstration of the power of God to deliver to the uttermost. Absolute holiness within and without, as the greatest spiritual insecticide, and a condition for Heaven is taught openly. MFM is a do-it-yourself Gospel Ministry, where your hands are trained to wage war and your fingers to fight.

ISBN 978-2947-54-7

Published by:
The PRESSHOUSE
MOUNTAIN OF FIRE AND MIRACLES MINISTRIES
Olasimbo Street, Onike (near Unilag 2nd Gate), P.O.Box 2990, Sabo, Yaba, Tel. 01-868766, Lagos, Nigeria.
E-Mail: mfm@micro.com.ng mfm@nigol.net.ng
Website: www.mountain-of-fire.com

www.ingramcontent.com/pod-product-compliance
Lightning Source LLC
Chambersburg PA
CBHW060857050426
42453CB00008B/996